Both E. John _____

Vera Ryan

Jean Bruneau

Margus Bruneau

Best Wishes

Arclan Ryan

St. John's

St. John's

SHERMAN HINES

Introduction by John C. Crosbie, P.C., Q.C., M.P.

NIMBUS PUBLISHING LIMITED

ST. JOHN'S

Nimbus Publishing Limited
P.O. Box 9301
Station A
Halifax
Nova Scotia
Canada
B3K 5N5

Canadian Cataloguing in Publication Data

Hines, Sherman.
St. John's

ISBN 0-920852-20-3

1. St. John's (Nfld.) - Description - Views.
I. Title.

FC2196.37.H56   917.18   C83-098010-5
F1124.5.S14H56

Second printing, 1985

Printed and bound in Hong Kong.

Colour separations, printing
and binding by Scanner Art Services Inc.
Toronto

Photographs taken with:
Pentax 6×7 using Ektachrome
Contax camera 35mm using Kodachrome

Caption consultant: Paul O'Neill,
author of *The Oldest City* and *A Seaport Legacy
— The Story of St. John's, Newfoundland*
(Press Porcepic, Erin, Ont.)

Introduction

St. John's! The oldest city in North America. The site where 400 years ago Sir Humphrey Gilbert first took possession of Newfoundland for the Queen and commenced the establishment of the British Empire. Newfoundland, the cornerstone of that empire and now the vital, resurgent soul of Eastern Canada!

St. John's! The capital of the former Dominion of Newfoundland and now Canada's tenth province. The site of the Colonial Building, the House of Assembly, the magnificent Roman Catholic and Anglican Cathedrals and of Signal Hill where Marconi received the first telegraph signal from across the Atlantic, now a national historic park.

The Harbour, landlocked, with the forbidding and spectacular entrance through the Narrows past the Battery and Fort Amherst. St. John's, still a fishing port with several hundreds of inshore fishermen, a major fish plant and trawler fleet, and still a haven from the storms of the North Atlantic for the fishing fleets of many nations.

The city is a mixture of the old and the new, with great awareness of its heritage and much done to preserve the old downtown residential areas amidst the new, modern suburbs.

A city renowned for its hospitality during the Second World War and renowned still as one of the friendliest and most hospitable receivers of guests and visitors on this globe.

The centre of the rebirth and flowering of the unique Newfoundland culture with a people interested in life, in living, in political affairs and in all human foibles, frailties and achievements.

I was born in the west end of St. John's and still have warm memories of the streetcar, the horse and sleigh and of the camaraderie of the St. John's 'Westender' and the 'corner' boy.

Today St. John's lies in the middle of an oil and gas development, just 190 miles from the shores of the harbour, and readies itself for the trials and wealth that lie not far over the horizon. Nightclubs, bars, pubs, disco's, restaurants, wine bars and funlovers abound.

From the city magnificent drives exist along the coastlines in every direction, with scenery unmatched in the western hemisphere. On those drives you will visit outports, coves, inlets, bights, harbours, tickles, sounds, runs, bays. You will see buoys, punts, dories, schooners, homes of unique charm and utility, fish flakes, stages, salt cod, fresh cod, cod tongues, sounds, flounders, flat fish, caplin rolling on the beaches, caplin frying in the frying pans, and caplin lying on the fields. You will taste fish and brewis, partridge, rabbit, moose, caribou, figgy duff, plum duff, blueberry duff and Dogberry wine.

Sherman Hines' book will be welcomed for the photographic panorama it presents of this historic and unique city. It complements handsomely the history of St. John's in two volumes authored by St. John's native, Paul O'Neill, several years ago.

This is my city, my home, my native isle. I welcome you to this wonderful book by Sherman Hines and to its coverage of the home we love so well.

John C. Crosbie, P.C., Q.C., M.P.
St. John's West

List of Plates

1. Sunlight breaks through the cloud and strikes the ocean, near the Narrows.

2. The lighthouse on the south side of the Narrows was, in earlier times, the site of Fort Amherst.

3. Fog shrouds the steep cliffs on the north side of the Narrows, the entrance to St. John's harbour.

4. A handsomely painted fishing vessel moored in the harbour on a foggy day.

5. Brightly painted houses are a distinctive feature of the Newfoundland landscape.

6. Along the north side of the harbour a cluster of wooden houses perch among the rocks on the steep slopes of the Battery.

7. View of the Narrows from the Battery. In war time a cable was laid across this channel to prevent enemy vessels slipping into the harbour.

8. Wharves and fish sheds along the Battery.

9. Affectionately named "The Rock", Newfoundland now stands as a land base for North Atlantic oil exploration.

10. The promise of new industry and the hope of new wealth makes an oil rig like this one a welcome sight in St. John's Harbour.

11. View of the waterfront of the core of the city from the north.

12. Across the harbour from the Southside at water level, the modern city of St. John's rises ready to dwarf the older images of a maritime economy.

13. Seagulls, guardians and scavengers – an integral part of every waterfront.

14, 15. Boats of many shapes and sizes have found shelter in St. John's Harbour for over four centuries. The fisheries, a major industry of Newfoundland, were the prime reason for seasonal, and later, permanent settlement.

16. Fishing vessels line the waterfront in front of Harbour Drive.

17. The Battery Motel commands a splendid westerly view of the city.

18. Traffic sweeps around the Royal Trust Building in downtown St. John's, casting surrealistic shafts of light.

19. Shaped like the bow of a boat, the harbour provides shelter from the harsh Atlantic.

20. Red, white and blue reflection on the water.

21. The Newfoundland flag, recently adopted by the province, was designed by artist Christopher Pratt.

22. The Roman Catholic Basilica stands sentinel over the city, a strong reminder of the Irish roots of many of its citizens.

23. City Hall, completed in 1970, was constructed of cast-in-place concrete, dramatizing the rugged terrain on which it is built.

24. A maze of colourful wooden houses rise up from the waterfront, the old in the foreground, the uniform patterns of the new above them.

25, 26, 27, 28. The architecture of St. John's is as varied as any city. In *The Domestic Architecture of St. John's* (Newfoundland Historical Society, 1974), the author, Shane O'Dea, refers to the strong Irish influence and to the cohesive elements that emerged in the rebuilding periods after the several fires in the nineteenth century that destroyed large sections of the city.

29. The Colonial Building, once the home of the Newfoundland parliament (1850-1934) and the provincial legislature (1949-1960), retains its palladian dignity although it no longer rings with the harangues of politicians and rioting mobs.

30. Memorial University, now nearly fifty years old, opened in 1925 with an enrollment of less than sixty students offering two years of study towards a B.A. or B.Sc. It has grown into a large university complex of over 11,000 students with a medical school, Fisheries Research Laboratory and extension services throughout Newfoundland and Labrador.

31, 32. Newfoundland War Memorial at Haymarket Square, King's Beach, was unveiled by Field Marshal Earl Haig in 1924.

33, 34. The Roman Catholic Basilica was erected under the supervision of Bishop Fleming, who laid the foundation stone in 1841 and celebrated the first mass there on January 6th, 1850.

35. St. John's is renowned for its friendly, easy-going atmosphere engendered by the people, descendants of the first fishermen and traders who settled here.

36. Railway tracks that run through Bowring Park, connect freight services across the province, and limited commuter traffic to nearby towns.

37, 38, 39, 40, 41, 42. Details from a tour of the harbour.

43. A sample of the rusting debris of twentieth century living.

44, 46. Factory ships, refrigerated trucks, centralized processing are some of the means employed to move large quantities of fish to distant markets.

45. Fisherman filleting his catch.

47. Along the waterfront on a typically foggy day, featuring Atlantic Place, office tower and shopping centre.

48. The photographer as artist catches this gull at the end of the day.

49. A view of the Battery at dusk.

50. The harbour front, from left to right, the Murray Premises, Bowrings, Atlantic Place and the Royal Trust Building.

51. Keeping fit at sunset on Signal Hill.

52. Masonic Hall.

53. Modern architecture is changing the skyline of St. John's. This is the Hotel Newfoundland.

54. Caribou statue in Bowring Park.

55. The interior of an antique shop.

56. A Newfoundland artist with a sample of his work.

57, 58. A restaurant with fine cooking displayed by the people who prepared it.

59 Houses and streets built before the age of the automobile, have to accommodate the hustle and bustle of modern city life.

60. Gower Street United Church, dating back to 1896, sits stunted now without its original spire, removed because of defects in its construction.

61. Government House, bedecked in this scene for Christmas, took three years to build (1825-1828) and exceeded the projected costs by over two hundred per cent to a total of over £100,000.

62. Confederation Building, built in 1959, is the seat of the provincial legislature and houses most of the offices of the various government departments.

63. Rennie's River is part of the scenic parkland of St. John's.

64. In the heart of the city this lattice-work fence protects a well-kept garden.

65. With an ear and half an eye to the world outside her window, a young girl sits like a framed portrait.

66. Ducks in Bowring Park.

67. Late on a summer's evening the quiet streets are a playground for the young.

69. Quidi Vidi village and lake on the outskirts of St. John's, is the site of the annual Regatta, purported to be the oldest continuing sports event in North America. Some of the oldest standing buildings of the area can be seen here, although many have fallen prey to modernization.

70. Looking up at Cabot Tower from a rooftop.

71. Cabot Tower was constructed on top of Signal Hill, five hundred feet above sea level, to commemorate the 400th anniversary of the discovery of Newfoundland by John Cabot and also Queen Victoria's Diamond Jubilee. It was opened in 1900.

72. View from Signal Hill.

73. St. John's, the harbour and the city, at dusk.

74. The golden sunset lights up a wheelhouse on a trawler.

75. Partially illuminated by the rising sun, these fishing boats make an early start on the day at the mouth of the harbour.

1

6

7

8

13

14

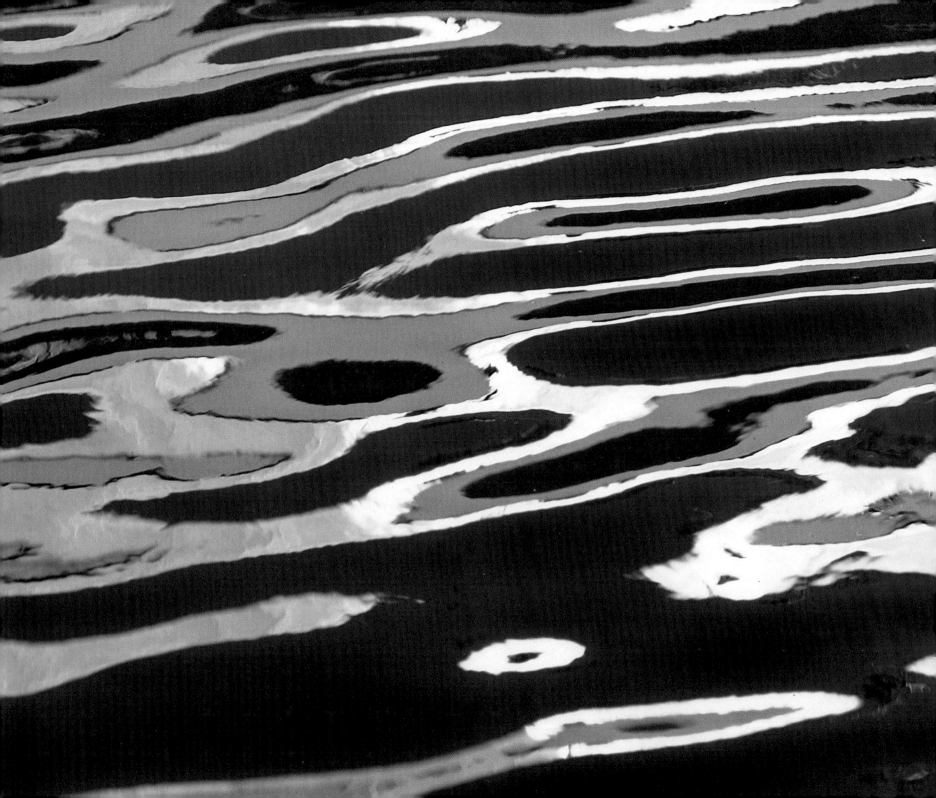

24

26

31

32

35

37

38

44

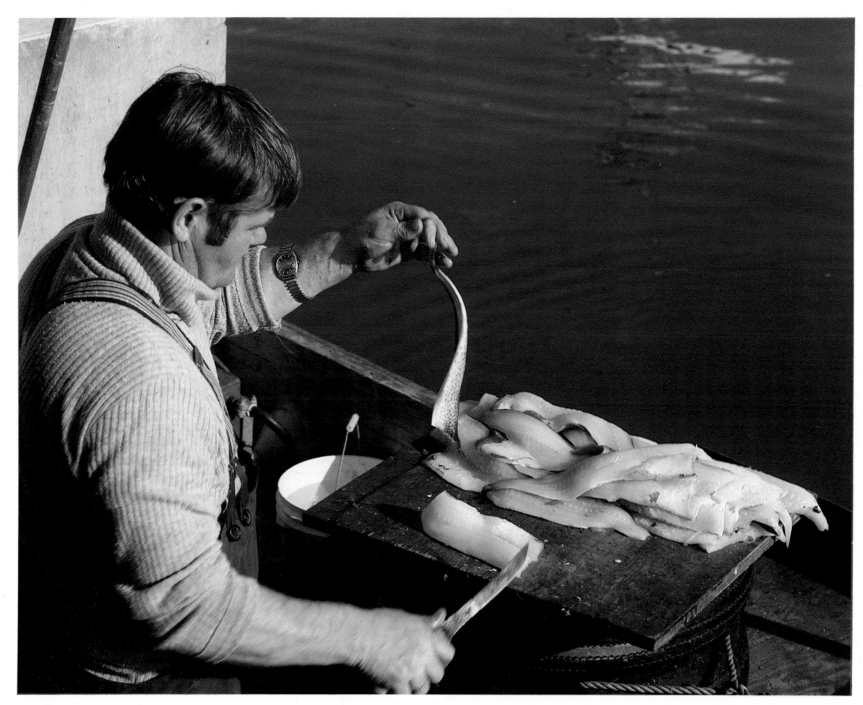

GREEN BAY TRANSPOR
ST. JOHN'S NFLD

57